Calligraphy for Beginners

Learn Calligraphy Alphabets, Lettering, Drawing, and More!

Table of Contents

Introduction	1
Chapter 1: What You Need to Know About Calligraphy	2
Chapter 2: Preparing Your Writing Tools	7
Ink	7
Paper	8
Pen	8
Ruler	9
Pen and nib holder	10
Lettering guides	10
Art table	11
Chapter 3: Improving Your Strokes	12
Chapter 4: Learning How to Do Calligraphy	17
Chapter 5: Calligraphic Characters Explained	21
Chapter 6: What to Do With Your Newfound Calligraphy Skills	25
Conclusion	28

**Copyright 2015 by Charlotte Pearce
- All rights reserved.**

This document is geared towards providing exact and reliable information in regards to the topic and issue covered. The publication is sold with the idea that the publisher is not required to render accounting, officially permitted, or otherwise, qualified services. If advice is necessary, legal or professional, a practiced individual in the profession should be ordered.

From a Declaration of Principles which was accepted and approved equally by a Committee of the American Bar Association and a Committee of Publishers and Associations.

In no way is it legal to reproduce, duplicate, or transmit any part of this document in either electronic means or in printed format. Recording of this publication is strictly prohibited and any storage of this document is not allowed unless with written permission from the publisher. All rights reserved.

The information provided herein is stated to be truthful and consistent, in that any liability, in terms of inattention or otherwise, by any usage or abuse of any policies, processes, or directions contained within is the solitary and utter responsibility of the recipient reader. Under no circumstances will any legal responsibility or blame be held against the publisher for any reparation, damages, or monetary loss due to the information herein, either directly or indirectly.

Respective authors own all copyrights not held by the publisher.

The information herein is offered for informational purposes solely, and is universal as so. The presentation of the information is without contract or any type of guarantee assurance.

The trademarks that are used are without any consent, and the publication of the trademark is without permission or backing by the trademark owner. All trademarks and brands within this book are for clarifying purposes only and are the owned by the owners themselves, not affiliated with this document.

Introduction

I want to thank you and congratulate you for purchasing the book, "Calligraphy for Beginners: Learn Calligraphy Alphabets, Lettering, Drawing, and More!".

This book contains proven steps and strategies on how to learn the various nuances of writing calligraphy. From the basics to the more advanced techniques, you'll learn everything you need to know on how to become the best calligrapher you can possibly become.

Thanks again for purchasing this book. I hope you enjoy it!

Chapter 1: What You Need to Know About Calligraphy

Because of the emergence of printing, computer programs, and other automated systems of writing, the art of writing using the hands have been somewhat forgotten by some. However, the truth is that handwriting has never gone out of style. This is because the human hand is capable of doing things any kind of machine will never be able to do. It is for this reason that after some time on the shadows, the art of calligraphy is once again emerging. Even better, by the looks of things, it looks like it's here to stay. Isn't today the best time to learn calligraphy? Before we get into that, we should first get into a short history lesson about the art of calligraphy.

Calligraphy was derived from 2 Greek words "kallos" and "graphe" which translates to "beautiful writing". In a nutshell, you can already derive the true meaning of calligraphy from this translation. A visual art that is related to writing, it is defined as the creation of artwork using letters, numbers, and other figures of language. The letters may or may not be legible, but they must be incorporated seamlessly and purposefully in the design. Calligraphic works are seen in both classic and modern art, and are considered to be works of art in and by itself.

Calligraphy has a long history that is as old as written language itself. In fact, just about every ancient civilization has its own form of calligraphy, as seen in ancient remains ranging from the walls of ruins to inscriptions of ancient paperwork. Western calligraphy is mainly known for the Latin script. Even during the fall of the Roman Empire, Latin influences in writing remained, as seen on the works of monasteries. During the middle ages, the Gothic script emerged, and was the script of choice even during the emergence of the printing press. In fact, Gothic was considered as the first typeface ever developed. Greek, Slavonic, and Russian calligraphy also exists, and are featured prominently in the countries where they are used.

Asia also has a very long history of calligraphic excellence. As the epicenter of some of the world's first civilizations, Asia is considered a hotbed for artistic writing. The first evidences of Chinese calligraphy are seen on ox scapulae and tortoise plastrons. As the written language of China developed, so is its obsession with calligraphy. Japanese and Korean calligraphy also shared some traits with the Chinese system. In these nations, handwriting was basically considered as both an art and a science. In India, calligraphic scripts were also uncovered, with the main medium of writing being smoke-treated palm leaves. Most of the scripts are written in Sanskrit, and Indian-inspired calligraphic works were also found in other nations such as Thailand and Tibet. Arabic calligraphy evolved together with Islam and the Arabic language. Mainly observed in Arab literature and mosques, calligraphy was considered as the most important form of Arabic art because of its direct link with Islam.

The emergence of the printing press has triggered the decline of calligraphy. There are many reasons for this decline, with the main one being the sheer practicality of just using typefaces for printed publications. But while calligraphy has entered a state of dormancy during this time, it never really went away.

A renewed interest in calligraphy emerged during the 19th century. Edward Johnston led this revival. Because of this, he was called the father of modern calligraphy. Influenced by the likes of William Hairston Cowlishaw and William Lethaby, Johnston eventually influenced a new generation of calligraphers such as Stanley Morrison, Eric Gill, and Graily Hewitt.

Even now, the art of calligraphy is still evolving. The students of Edward Johnston eventually taught themselves, adding their own inputs and insights into the craft. It is thru their work where a renewed interest in calligraphy exploded. Even casual writers are trying to learn the craft, which is always a good sign. Even in the midst of the computer age, people see the value in artistic writing. Some use it as a means of making a living. Others use it as a means for expressing their artistic side. Even some of the fonts we see on online programs are inspired by calligraphic works. These all show that calligraphy as an art is alive and well.

While it may seem like it's a craft reserved for those who have a feel for it, the fact is that anyone can learn how to do good calligraphy. Think of it this way: even the experts started from scratch, so it's not like you're alone on that regard. With the information found in this guide, you'll learn how to do your own calligraphic artwork. While I cannot personally guarantee that you will be a pro immediately (your progress would still be up to you), I will give you everything you need to know so you can get started on the right track.

Chapter 2: Preparing Your Writing Tools

Calligraphy, just like any kind of art form, is highly reliant on the skill and creativity of the artist. Whatever comes out of his mind and how he projects it using his skills is the main determinant of the quality of a specific work. However, for artists of any level, it wouldn't hurt if they have the appropriate tools for the trade. Even as a beginner, it would help if you have access to calligraphy tools. More than just having access to writing tools, it is also important that you understand how to use them right. You'll learn both of these things right here.

Ink

The ink you'll use is important for creating solid calligraphic material. The quality of your ink would determine if your writing would be silky smooth or it would resemble a dirty picture. For basic writing, you can use traditional inks such as black India ink, Chinese stick ink, and lamp-black water color. The good news is that these inks usually work for different kinds of writing surfaces. Depending on the surface you'll be writing on, you have the choice of either using a water-based or an oil-based ink. You can also get inks of different colors if you desire. As a beginner, it's best to stick with one color and then expand with color options as you increase your mastery.

Paper

The canvas you use is crucial when it comes to creating art. Pick the wrong paper and you'll never get the results you wish. It might seem overwhelming on the surface because there are all kinds of paper available. Your usual printing or bond paper would not cut it because they have a tendency to "bleed" ink. While these papers are good enough for practicing, it's not going to cut it when you're already creating your masterpieces. It's best to get paper with enough thickness to support calligraphy ink without bleeding. For basic lettering projects, it's best to go for paper with 190gsm weight. If you'll be using extensive designs, better go for papers with weight equal or greater than 300gsm.

Pen

Your pen is a very important part of your arsenal. After all, you write with it. While other writing tools can be used such as quills and brushes, the standard equipment for modern calligraphers is the fountain pen. The type of pen you'll use depends on the work you will do and your writing style. For those who are interested in making fine lines, getting pens with fine nibs would be your best option. Getting a coarser nib would do for those who want thicker lines and/or those who have the tendency to draw fast. You can purchase a pen with replaceable nibs or just purchase multiple pens with different nibs. As you progress further, you'll learn how to use specific nibs. At the same time, with time and familiarity, you'll figure out which nibs you are most comfortable with.

Ruler

This is a must have tool for those who are still getting their feet wet. The use of a ruler would ensure that you'll get the proportions of your writing right. While you can always start out using graphic paper, there would eventually be a time that you must progress into using clear paper. Using a ruler would help you out in proportions until you get familiar with writing even without a guide. A standard ruler should be good for you. Make sure to get a clear one so you can see what's beneath. Also, I would recommend that you get a graphic ruler. It has numerous graduations that would help you in getting more precise measurements. As for ideal length, anywhere from 6 to 24 inches is good.

Pen and nib holder

A holder, while not necessary for creating artwork by itself, would come very handy when you are working on more complex projects wherein you'll be switching pens and nibs. For your convenience, I would recommend that you get a pen and nib holder. Finding one should be easy. You can find one at your local art store or even improvise one if you're feeling creative.

Lettering guides

One of the hallmarks of calligraphy is the freedom to improvise. Of course, while you are free to be creative, it won't hurt if you have a formal reference point. This is where getting a lettering guide would help you. At first, it may seem too tricky to follow. However, once you get the hang of it, you'll recognize that it's an incredibly useful tool for refining your lettering technique. You can get these guides on your local art store and you can also search for printable guidelines online. It must be noted that lettering guides printed on standard paper might bleed ink.

Art table

Some people would prefer drawing on a traditional table, but we would recommend that you invest on a good art table. It would help in keeping your canvas properly in place. At the same time, as long as you maintain the table well, it would give your canvas a clean and even place to sit in. This would help in giving you the best artwork possible. The right table would also enable you to draw virtually anywhere. Find a good art table and it shall be your buddy in calligraphy for a long time.

Having a complete set of accessories does not guarantee that you'll become a great calligrapher. However, investing on these would greatly help you as you discover and develop your calligraphic skills. Not only would these items make your life easier, but it would also enable you to maximize whatever skills you have at any specific moment. It's very possible that you'll be getting more equipment when you start to learn more about

Chapter 3: Improving Your Strokes

There are many ways to approach learning of calligraphy. One of the best approaches out there is to develop your hand skill. After all, you cannot create excellent calligraphy without mastering the skills necessary to control the pen. By taking control of your hands, you'll take a significant step towards becoming a great calligrapher. This chapter would focus on your hands, more specifically on how you can improve your strokes for better calligraphy. This is a step-by-step approach on how you can refine your overall calligraphic technique.

1. Analyze your handwriting- Improvement begins when you start recognizing specific problems with your penmanship. There are many ways to do this, but I'll give you a simple way to do it. All you need to do is to write something. It may be a paragraph, it may be a sentence, or it may be a single calligraphic figure. After writing, analyze the flaws present. Flaws include shaky lines and curves. There may be rough corners. There might be improper spacing and proportions. There might be irregular slanting. Take note of all these errors.

You'll need this information once you start practicing.

2. Look for inspiration- When trying to change something, having the right inspiration would definitely help. One source of viable inspiration would be checking out both calligraphic works and handwriting styles. Of course, when you see a style that you like, you would do your best to imitate it. Before you know it, you'll find yourself imitating it, taking you closer to the results that you desire. Make a copy of each style you feel is feasible for you to learn. It may or may not approximate your writing style at the moment, but still get it. You may not adapt the entire style altogether, but you can acquire specific traits you want to add to your repertoire.

3. Improve your pen grip- This may sound elementary, but the way you grip your writing tool determines how good your writing would be. The correct way of holding a pen or brush is by holding it between your thumb and index finger. If your hands are small or you just prefer a wider grip, you can also include the middle finger in supporting the pen. The pen should be resting against either in between the index and thumb or at the knuckle of the index. Use the thumb to hold into the bottom third of the pen. The grip should be just right, not too tight and not too loose. A grip that's too tight would result to limited pen movement. A grip that's too loose would result to lack of stability.

4. Improve your writing mechanics- Specific muscle groups are at work when you are writing. Training these muscles to work in proper coordination is an important factor in determining one's writing ability. Most of the time, we write only using our hand and wrist. The correct way of writing actually involves both the arm and shoulder. Instead of drawing using your hand, modify your approach by using your arm and shoulder to conjure letters and images together with your hand. One good way to practice this is to write in the air. While holding a pen, write letters, sentences, and figures in the air. This would train your arm and shoulder muscles to move together with your hand. Such an approach can vastly improve your calligraphic ability.

5. Practice the basics- This step is like going back to preschool. While this step may sound childish, the logic here is to refine your basic handwriting skills. When your fundamental writing mechanics are solid, going for more advanced writing exercises would be much easier to do. On a blank piece of paper, you can practice writing letters first, taking note of your personal progress while you're at it. Once you feel your letter-crafting skills are solid and consistent enough, proceed to completing words, sentences, and then paragraphs. With practice and familiarity, you'll acquire a newfound mastery of handwriting. You can also practice with basic shapes to improve your drawing skills. Utilizing a directional chart can potentially be helpful in this regard.

6. Use your hands whenever you can- Because of the presence of digital writing systems, handwriting has become more or less a forgotten skill. If you are intending to become a calligrapher, you must never forget to use your hands while writing. Just like most skills, handwriting is a skill that takes practice, repetition, and familiarity to master. One of the best ways to master something is through practical application. If your hands are properly trained to write and draw, it can execute more creative works. The goal here is to keep your hands engaged as much as possible.

Learning to maximize the power of your hands is important for improving your writing and drawing skills. Beyond any accessory, your hands are the most important tools in calligraphy. Because of this, proper training and continuous practice is essential to become great in this craft. Once you've mastered hand control and basic writing and drawing technique, you're ready to go to the next level of calligraphic learning.

Chapter 4: Learning How to Do Calligraphy

Now we are entering the fun part of your training. On the earlier parts of this book, we tackled how the right set of tools and an improved mastery of your hands can help you become the best calligrapher possible. The reason why I brought up those topics first is because I feel it's essential that you get both of these in order before jumping into the more advanced lessons. Calligraphy is a complex skill to master in itself, so it's important that you come in training ready and armed. Now, I can confidently say you are confident and armed for some serious calligraphy training.

Here are some tips I can share with you:

1. Understanding the thick-and-thin effect- The combination of thick and thin lines makes letters looking much more impressive. It may seem difficult on the surface, but with the right nib and proper hand action, you can master this effect and use it to your advantage. There are 2 things you must remember to properly execute the thick-and-thin effect. First, you'll need to keep the pen angle constant so to not disturb the writing pattern already established. Second, remember that you must keep lines parallel with each other and curves must remain even. It would take some practice to get this right on a regular basis, but you can do it.

2. Keep your pen at a constant angle- This is one fundamental skill all calligraphers must master. They MUST keep their pens at a constant angle at all times. When using pencils and conventional pens, the convention is to change the angle of the writing device to change up the shade thickness. That's something you don't have to do if you're using a calligraphy pen. The nibs of your pen are designed in such a way that the shading thickness varies depending on the direction of your stroke, not on the angle of your pen. The exact angle you can use depends on the type of script you're creating or the type of nib you're using. As a rule of thumb, the angle should be kept anywhere between 30 to 60 degrees. Test your nibs first to determine the ideal angle for a particular project.

3. Apply just the right pressure- The pressure you put in between the pen and paper should be just right. Too little pressure means your nib would not make full contact with the paper. Too much pressure would cause too much application of ink and may even result to damage to the nib. You wouldn't like either one to happen as it would mess with the overall quality of your work. To do this, make the nib gently touch the paper. With your hand barely touching the paper, guide the pen as you write, keeping the pen at a constant angle at all times. Do not lean too heavily on your hand, arm, elbow, or shoulder. Not only would this put too much pressure on the nib, but it can also be very exhausting.

4. Keep your nib fixed- This is basically an offshoot of steps 1 and 2. Aside from maintaining a constant angle as you write, it is also important that you keep your nib at a fixed position. This means that as you write, you must not rotate your pen as it would mess up everything. Doing this is actually not as hard as you may initially think. There are only a few adjustments you must do to get this done. First, you'll need to keep the pen fixed at a specific position. It should not be too hard as long as your grip and writing form is stable. Second, make a conscious effort to keep your nib at a fixed position at all times. Some may have the habit of moving/rotating the pen around while writing. Such habit must be eliminated when doing calligraphic work.

5. Keep lines parallel- The ability to draw parallel lines is a skill calligraphers of all levels must possess. It doesn't matter if the lines are horizontal, vertical, diagonal, or curved. A properly executed calligraphic work would show proper proportions in each line. One way to ensure this is by keeping lines parallel. Keeping your lines parallel is all a matter of keeping your pen stable at all times. Get your grip right and make sure that your nib is kept at a fixed position. Simple as that, your lines will stay parallel, no matter what the font or surface.

Those are some of the most basic things you must master as a student of calligraphy. Holding your pen the right way, applying the correct pressure, holding the nib in place at all times, and keeping the lines parallel are skills you must learn in all levels of calligraphic practice. Never forget these and you shall never be lost while constructing your crafts.

Chapter 5: Calligraphic Characters Explained

When people talk about calligraphy, one of the first things that come to mind is the use of specific letter systems. Calligraphy is always related to systematic writing, often utilizing a distinct letter system for executing scripts, logos, and everything else in between. There are all kinds of fonts out there you can use. You can use specific lettering guides to check out what they are. You can even improvise your own lettering system if you have the skill for it. Here are some of the most popular styles of fonts in the calligraphic world. In fact, a lot of fonts are actually inspired by these classics.

1. Roman- This style basically encapsulates almost all forms of Western calligraphy. As the world's most widely used alphabet, it is the most ubiquitous form of letters you can see. It also has the distinction of having the most number of variations. As it's used in virtually every part of the planet, calligraphers from all over the world have put their own unique twist to writing Roman characters. During the time it first emerged, Roman calligraphy was created as a "smart casual" way of relaying written information. There are sub-variations of the Roman style of writing such as the use of Rustic capitals. Learning this is simple because of sheer familiarity. The Roundhand style is perhaps the simplest and best example of Roman-style writing.

2. Gothic- Essentially a derivative of the Roman alphabet system, Gothic characters have a formal feel to it when you read them. A positive about learning this font is that while it looks complex on the surface, it's actually relatively simple to recreate. This form of lettering mainly constitutes parallel straight lines, making it easier to draw. Even better, because it looks more complex than it actually is, you can use this style to impress just about anyone. You can first focus in drawing the main elements of the letters before proceeding to the smaller details. You'll be surprised to see that with practice, you can easily learn how to write in Gothic.

3. Greek- As one of the oldest forms of written language in the world, Greek letters would always hold a special place in calligraphy.

Derived from the more ancient Phonecian alphabet, it is considered by many as a direct ascendant of the Roman alphabet used worldwide today. Greek letters are still used a lot in various applications, and have become a favorite among calligraphers who want to write texts with a little twist. Writing in Greek should be treated like writing in Roman. The letters and symbols might have slightly changed, but the execution for writing them remains the same.

4. Arabic-The Arabic language and alphabet are extensively used around the world thanks to the continued presence of Islam. The Arabic language, both in its oral and written form, is treated with reverence by Muslims and those who live in Arab-speaking places. Needless to say, Arabic is also very popular with calligraphers from around the world. Like most Eastern alphabets, writing Arabic is a bit tricky unless you actually have a background in using it. Different scripts are used for Arabic. The most popular ones include Kufic, Naskh, Thuluth, and Diwani. Each script is different from the other in many ways, from the shape of the letters to the orientation of writing in space. You can study each script individually, but we recommend that you start first with the basic ones.

5. Chinese- Some scholars consider Chinese calligraphy to be a completely different discipline in itself, as its alphabet does not resemble anything like in other countries around the world. Still, calligraphy has a central importance in Chinese culture as it's considered to be among the "arts". There are different styles of writing in this writing, with some examples including Lishu and Kaishu. Traditional Chinese calligraphy involve the use of brush, paper, ink, and inkstone, collectively called as the "Four Treasures of the Study". While the traditional way of writing and drawing Chinese characters is still valued, doing calligraphy using modern calligraphic tools is now being embraced.

There are other calligraphic styles found around the world. Those are just 5 of the best examples around. Due to different reasons ranging from popularity to complexity, mastering any (or even all) of these calligraphic styles would immensely benefit you as an artist. Try to learn them and have fun doing it!

Chapter 6: What to Do With Your Newfound Calligraphy Skills

By now, you have developed your calligraphy skills to the point that you can now show it off with confidence. But now that you have learned how to do calligraphy, what would you do next? Of course, doing nothing should not be an option. There are a lot of things you can do with your calligraphic ability. Here are some of the best suggestions I can give you on how you can take advantage of your skills and stay improving at the same time.

1. Keep practicing- There is always room for improvement. This should be your mentality when you're trying to learn anything. Constantly working on your calligraphy would result to improvements. In fact, even the best in this craft constantly practice. It is during your practice time where you fortify your strengths and work on your weaknesses as a calligrapher. It would be wise if you practice too. Allot even a miniscule amount of your free time into calligraphic practice and you shall be good in no time.

2. Try variations- You might have already mastered a specific font, but it doesn't have to end there. There are numerous variations with each form of writing. It might be in the way the characters are written. It might be on how specific elements are written in the text. It might be on how the details are set up on the background. Successfully incorporating variations increases the diversity of your work. At the same time, it also gives you more ideas on how you can polish your personal style.

3. Create your own crafts- Calligraphy is often used in different crafts. The best way to put your calligraphic skills to the test is to use them to actually make actual artwork. There are different crafts and handiworks that utilize calligraphy as a means for adding style. Anything from pottery to tattoos, posters to certificates, calligraphy is a versatile way to add design to just about anything. The artwork you produce can become part of your portfolio and might even be used for profit.

4. Accept calligraphic services- Because calligraphy is considered a skill, being a calligrapher can be considered as a skilled profession. Because of this, it would be wise if you would offer your services as a calligrapher. Not only is this a great way to make some money, but it is also a great way to challenge your skills. You can offer your services to both online and offline clients. Currently, the demand for calligraphers is high. It would be wise to take advantage of that.

5. Create your own style- One of the best things you can have as an artist is to have your own style. Getting your own style does not happen overnight, as it takes both insight and experience to figure out which style fits for you. As you continue doing calligraphy, you'll learn about the things you can do. At the same time, you'll recognize which technique or variation fits you. Combine knowledge with creativity and you'll be developing your own style in no time.

Conclusion

Thank you again for purchasing this book!

I hope this book was able to help you to learn everything you need to become a great calligrapher.

The next step is to use the tips mentioned in this book so you can continue improving your calligraphic skills! The learning should never end with this book.

Finally, if you enjoyed this book, please take the time to share your thoughts and post a review on Amazon. It'd be greatly appreciated!

Thank you and good luck!